HODGEPODGE

HODGEPODGE

A Random Collection of Poems
and Songs Like Nothin' You've Ever Read

JERRY D. JACKSON

Printed in the United States of America

ISBN 979-8-89114-248-0 (sc)
ISBN 979-8-89114-249-7 (e)

Library of Congress Control Number: 2025923520

2026.01.14

MainSpring Books
5901 W. Century Blvd
Suite 750
Los Angeles, CA, US, 90045

www.mainspringbooks.com

PREFACE

After years of writing and rewriting my poems and songs, the time has come for me to present them to you, the reader. In my short seventy-nine years of life, I have experienced many wonderful things with some even bordering on horrible. What you're about to read are my attempts to express my life through the written word, poetry, to be exact. As for the subject matter, for me, a poem was created when an idea popped into my head. If I was driving around at the time, I would simply pull over, jot down a few notes, and get back on the road. Later, to sit down and work on that idea to see if something was there.

Other hints would come to me at various times of the day or night in the form of sights, sounds, and of course, from all the different memories we store away back in the dark recesses of our brains. I truly hope that one or more of them will call back to your memory an event or happening in your life that brought you some laughter, happiness or maybe even some joy.

Thank you for buying my book and I really hope that you can find a way to apply at least one of my poems or songs to your life and come away with some very good memories.

Jerry D Jackson

CONTENTS

Poems Relating to Marriages and Relationships

Poems With a Religious Theme

Poems of an Adventurous Nature

Poems of a Silly & Funny Nature

Poems Inspired by The Old West

Inspirational Poems

Poems of a General Nature

My Songs

EYE OF THE NEEDLE

The sun peaks over the horizon,
On its trip across the sky.
Lives will be changed today,
Some are born, while others die.

The times continue to change,
To what we simply don't know.
As we draw closer to the end,
The signs He'll begin to show.

Coming down throughout the ages
Man has talked about this day.
Does he latch onto a comets tail,
On earth, is he allowed to stay?

Man's quest for endless knowledge,
Takes us further from the King.
Over time, people have learned,
It is He to whom angels sing.

The eye of the needle grows smaller,
As their heads begin to swell.
Unless they choose the narrow road,
With Satan, their souls will dwell.

There's no need for endless worry,
As we face each blessed day.
I know when He died for us,
Our sins He took away.

HELL

W hat's it like to be in hell?
Some will never know.
It's not a place for the pure of heart,
It's a place they'll never go.

Hell is reserved for the vicious,
Where pure evil will reside.
You can try to blame others, but,
You're going with no place to hide.

You can rob, cheat, lie and steal,
Keep doing what you love to do.
Satan is standing in the door of hell,
Just waiting there for you.

Hell is a place void of laughter,
Where agony will always prevail.
There's torment, pain, and gnashing of teeth,
Why else would they call it hell?

So, enjoy yourselves, sons of Satan,
Go ahead and have your fun.
God lets you have it your way,
But your time is nearly done.

Satan wins over millions of souls,
But he forgot just one small thing.
You don't mess around with God almighty,
And Jesus, the King of Kings.

IF HEAVEN COULD WAIT

I know if heaven could wait,
I'd spend more time with you.
But we have nothing to say,
About the things God will do.

The life you had was amazing,
And you helped the people out.
You gave so freely of yourself,
Never raising your voice to shout.

You were known throughout the area
And greeted wherever you went.
You were loved by all the people,
Who were surely heaven sent.

You gave your life to Jesus,
Things, you did in His name.
But as the world forever changes,
Our lives are never the same.

If only heaven could wait,
Such a blessing you'd be to us.
But once God calls your name,
In Him, you'll place your trust.

THAT SILENT NIGHT

As I listen to the songs of Christmas
Pure joy fills my heart.
I know why the songs were written,
And how they got their start.

The songs of Christmas tell the story,
Of a special time of year.
They remind us of a blessed night,
As a star shown bright and clear.

Jesus was born to Joseph and Mary.
On a night much like this.
Satan opened his book of tricks,
But he still couldn't make Him his.

Satan tried to defeat God's plan,
So that Christ would not be born.
What he discovered on that silent night,
Let others be forewarned.

Jesus Christ is the King of Kings
And stands second to none.
Born of a virgin in Bethlehem
God's plan was not yet done.

As our savior died on the cross,
He took our sins away.
Later, the world would praise His name,
On every Christmas Day.

THE SON

The promise He made many years ago,
Has grown a little since then.
The people looked up and prayed to God,
And He sent us Him.

He was born to Joseph and Mary.
He did things money couldn't buy.
Three wise men searched for him
Being led by a star in the sky.

He never had gold or fine clothing,
And palaces, He passed on the street.
Of all the people who walked the earth
He's the one we all want to meet.

Jesus was sent to earth one day,
To save mankind from sin.
As He walked and preached the gospel,
He would defeat death, and then,

He was buried in the tomb of a friend,
His work on earth was done.
Jesus had completed His time on earth,
The Father was proud of the Son.

Jesus of Nazareth was the King of Kings
And he would always be with man.
Despite the attempts of tyrants and such
There's nothing that will stop God's plan.

CHOICES

God in Heaven created all things,
And gave humanity a choice.
For those who fail to choose wisely,
Who will be their voice?

One of the blessings He gave us,
Even now, is called free will.
If the choices we make, harm others,
We'll answer for them still.

You choose the person you marry,
And only you should have the right.
Your marriage should last forever,
But the newness, for just a night.

It's your choice to be a mother,
And no one should interfere.
You choose your sexual preference,
And many come out each year.

Dieting is a choice you make,
As is the place you live.
You make the choice of what to keep,
Or you can choose instead to give.

Think of the choices made each day,
But where do we look to begin?
Your friends know you're with child,
And to kill it would be a sin.

In all things worldly, you make choices,
And He gave you this life to live.
If someone chooses to harm you
Like Jesus, you'll choose to forgive.

THE RESCUE

As we live but often struggle,
To make the best of our time
Many of us will live and die,
With nothing we'll ever call, mine.

For me, however, I'm a satisfied man,
And I'm always ready to say.
Why some of us are allowed to live,
While others are taken away.

It's difficult for us to imagine,
Seeing a friend without his wife.
One was taken from the jaws of death,
The other one lost her life.

Not one of them was able,
To say thank you at the time.
But thinking back over the years
Thanks, was not on their minds.

I was so happy in knowing,
That for me, I'd done my best.
We placed him in the hands of God,
And He took care of the rest.

Our God will rescue some from Satan,
Who's the father of all lies.
Eternal life with God almighty,
Where each should forever strive.

THE BELL

W hen the bell tolls for me
I'll be on my way home.
I've waited all these many years,
And have never been alone.

Yes, God's watched over me,
Before I was ever conceived.
And by going back to Him
That's proof, I wasn't deceived.

Every new day of my life,
A test, I had to pass.
Bad things were thrown at me,
But I knew I could outlast.

The devil did his very best,
And I failed time and again.
But by the grace of God
I'll spend my life with Him.

If my life was but a guide
You'd have learned a thing or two.
If you decide to kneel and pray,
He'll take great care of you.

When the bell tolls for me
I'll be on my way home.
I've waited all these many years,
And have never been alone.

I COME TO YOU

With my eyes wide open - I come to you.
With my heart just a'thumping - I come to you.
With the congregation smiling - I come to you.
To join the family of God - my choice is to be with you.

Because I'm a sinner - I come to you.
With my soul on the line - I come to you.
Because you died for me - I come to you.
To join the family of God - I come to you.

I come to you freely without coercion from any man.
I come to you willingly as only a free people can.
I come to you openly as the Bible tells us to.
To join the family of God and to be closer to you.

With my butterflies churning - I come to you.
With the promise of salvation - I come to you.
And because I love you so - I come to you.
For all the promises you made - I come to you.

With family by my side - I come to you.
As my church family waits - I come to you.
With the preacher at the ready - I come to you.
To join the family of God - I come to you.

I come to you freely without coercion from any man.
I come to you willingly as only a free people can.
I come to you openly as the Bible tells us to.
To join the family of God and to be closer to you.

THE CRAVING

He was born into slavery, on a cold winter's day,
Never tasting freedom 'til his life slipped away.
He toiled for the man from early day 'till night.
And considered running, but the master was a fright.

He learned of the country his family came from,
The story being passed from father to son.
They talked proudly of the things they once knew,
Like floating down a river in a handmade canoe.

So, freedom is a word he knew something about,
But if he spoke the word, the master would shout.
He listened and learned about things to do,
One day, he'd be free, somehow, he just knew.

His craving for freedom hit a high, one day,
When he heard of a man with things to say.
His heart grew happy, and his eyes could see,
As Jesus told the crowd how it would be.

He was finally free from the pain and sin,
And free from the wicked and evil men.
He was free from all the sadness and crying,
And free from the sickness and from dying.

For on that day, he was free at last,
And from that day forward, he had no past.
After hearing the words, He had to say,
His soul was in heaven with Jesus that day.

BELIEVE IN ME

M arvelous things await us there,
In the home we're going to receive.
Jesus left us many years past,
And told us in what to believe.

Believe in me, and you'll receive
The gift of eternal life.
Can you imagine living in a world,
With no pain, misery, or strife?

Believe in me, and you'll receive,
A body that is lean and bold.
Imagine having a body like that,
One, that will never grow old.

Believe in me, and I'll give you sight,
If the eyes you have are blind.
Imagine the joy you're going to have,
When you see Him for the very first time.

Believe in me, and I'll raise the dead,
Lazarus, was called from his tomb.
Though he was dead, his family believed
And tonight, he'll sleep in his room.

I say to all who believe in Jesus,
You'll live with Him in heaven.
If you choose the other, all is lost,
As your soul to Satan, is given.

FREE WILL

I was drawn to this moment,
By what, I didn't know.
Some told me it was destiny,
Others said it wasn't so.

Our free will is a good thing,
We say the things we must.
God gave it to us willingly,
It's ours to make it or bust.

He always leaves a door open,
When trouble stares at our face.
There's no need to take a life,
Or even enter their space.

So, you wanted to be a lawyer,
But you never took your test.
You chose to be a teacher instead,
Trying to help the very best.

So, the job didn't go your way,
And she wasn't looking for you.
Your life won't end tomorrow,
If you stop what you're going to do.

You can put your trust in Jesus,
As He gave His life for man.
Your soul will then be at peace,
If you accept His ultimate plan.

BELIEVE IN JESUS

From the beginning, we've had free will,
To make decisions about life.
He gave it to us for right or wrong,
Good people will have less strife.

When you believe in the Lord Jesus Christ,
His blessings will come to you.
But if you choose to ignore His teachings,
I'd hate to be in your shoes.

Believe in Jesus with an ounce of faith,
And obey Him the best you can.
Imagine the pain He suffered for us,
As He paid for the sins of man.

All things good come from Jesus,
The bad, from the son of perdition.
Eternal life awaits true believers,
While death is Satan's condition.

Why would you choose to live with Satan,
When you know what awaits you there?
Those who believe will be with Jesus,
Where the chances of dying are rare.

Consider the facts before you decide,
The wrong one leads to strife.
If you partake in the second death,
You'll lose your mortal life.

IT MATTER'S NOT

God loves you just as you are,
He loves the good, and the bad.
Get a job or go to school,
With God, you'll never be sad.

Riches come in different forms,
Like faith, family, and love.
It matters not about your friends
Or that life gives you a shove.

There's a place in Heaven for us,
And Jesus will take us there.
Don't you tell us what to do,
Just turn to Him if you dare.

It matters not where you work.
Just pay your way and don't take.
Government slaves are takers,
Skilled workers sell what they make.

In life, we want the good things
Like family, friends, and love.
What a happy life we'll have
When blessed from our God above.

No need for you to worry,
If God is with you today.
Choose wisely your decisions,
And think when you have your say.

F ar beneath the melting ice
Lies a seed that yearns to grow.
But not until the springtime sun
Will the blossom feel its glow.

The sun gives life to many things,
And people need it to live.
Providing light and warmth to boot,
The sun never forgives.

Crops in the fields need it to grow,
And man, for the light, it gives.
Oceans take in the heat of the day,
So that life within it lives.

People still need the son of God,
To provide light for their souls.
Without His light to guide them home
Their lives will never be whole.

He gives life where life is not,
And hope where there is none.
He gives joy where truly needed,
And God is seen in the Son.

Be it the sun or the Son of God,
We need them both to live.
If either one is taken away
This earth has nothing to give.

STAY WITH THE SON

As I walk through the valley of shadows and doubt,
My faith I put in the Lord.
Then, as I slip and slide through life,
He corrects us with a tongue like a sword.

He was tempted by Satan but never gave in.
He searched for John, who would baptize him.
He traveled around, His disciples to find,
That followed Him as He preached to mankind.

He's our comforter and soothes troubled hearts.
He's our Master and has been from the start.
Jesus ascended, a mansion to prepare.
Upon His return, all eyes will stare.

I've sinned, as all of mankind will do.
I was forgiven when I asked Him to.
The savior is my Lord, and I look to Him.
People seek Him before their lights dim.

Wait no longer before you call His name.
He's always there, never causing you shame.
The Lord is our shepherd and looks out for you.
He corrects us by giving a push or two.

Keep your values solid, and do what is right.
Teach them to pray before going to bed at night.
Keep God in your life, keep Him number one.
Never let evil creep in, stay true to the Son.

A POOR BOY

I was born and raised a poor boy.
With nothing to put in the bank.
A place to stay with love galore,
My parents were there to thank.

Worldly possessions I had none,
But I collected what I could.
Rocks or string, all sorts of things,
I prized them as I should.

But nothing we owned had value,
As we understand value today.
My treasures made me feel good,
That I collected along the way.

Kids in the hood got out to play,
A game called, "Roll-a-Bat."
But kids today are stuck inside,
And never play like that.

What good is money anyway
If you never have real fun?
If you go somewhere and flaunt it,
You better be ready to run.

I'm just a poor ole country boy,
With devoted neighbors and friends.
Special treasures I stored away,
Will be there to the end.

I CRIED A TEAR

The older I got, the less we talked,
During the time I lived at home.
But when I left to spread my wings,
We talked before she was gone.

I cried a tear when I got the news,
That mama had passed away.
I never had a chance to say good-bye,
And I miss her to this day.

Mom took care of her children,
Her needs were always last.
She always made plans for the future,
Never being concerned with the past.

Her motherly love was instinctive
And you could see it evermore.
One day, I left to seek my fortune,
Never knowing what laid in store.

The skills mama gave me were impeccable,
And my womanhood was something to see.
Mama told me all about life,
Except how lonely it could be.

I wish now we'd talked more often,
Like true friends often do.
Maybe then I could've said,
Thanks more often, and, I love you.

THE PHYSICIAN

The physician is the one who cures our pains.
The physician is known by many names.
The physician sees you in your finest clothes.
The physician and stylist are the two who knows.

The physician is a person you can talk to.
The physician stays busy with things to do.
The physician removes things you don't need.
The physician laughs at what boys do with a seed.

The physician doesn't worry about your soul.
The physician tries to keep your body whole.
The physician can be a woman or man.
The physician always does the best they can.

The physician can have a good life at home.
The physician might spend many hours alone.
The physician is a friend of young and old.
The physician's stethoscope is always cold.

The physicians of old did all they could do.
The physicians today do what they have to.
The physicians of old practiced from the heart.
The physicians today view money from the start.

The physician, it seems, gets sued every day.
The physician today studies hard to stay.
The physician today knows what's in store.
The physician today faces problems galore.

MY BROTHER

My brother was older than me,
According to our mom and dad.
My three sisters, treated me well,
He was the only brother I had.

Every time I did something wrong,
He was there to guide me home.
When our friends wanted to play,
He would always bring me alone.

Everybody looked up to him,
As he stood about six feet tall.
Tall or not, he couldn't help me,
When I ran to the street for a ball.

Now, I watch over him each day,
Looking down, I can see him grow.
If I had to do it all over again,
I would still want it to be so.

In this dimension, I know all things,
I wish I could tell you why.
I know you'd find it hard to believe,
If you could see it with your eyes.

I can't tell you how long it's been,
But rejoice that I'm not alone.
I know that when his time comes,
I'll be taking my brother home.

A BUSY MAN

I think of myself as a busy man,
Because I have a lot to do.
I never liked just sitting around,
When I could take on a job or two.

When the grass was tall, I had it cut,
The borders I shaped and trimmed.
But don't forget that honey-do list,
It hasn't changed since God knows when.

He's always been a busy man,
People tell me time and again.
If you take away one of his jobs,
You'll hear a lot from him.

He never takes the time to rest,
Because he's working all the time.
If he's not working on a job of his,
He'll be working on one of mine.

He's always checking his "to-do" list.
For work, he can do in the yard.
And if he's not taking in lots of tea
Then he can't be working that hard.

Busy men make good husbands,
Since you always know where they are.
There's never a need for you to worry,
If they're lost, they can't be far.

THE REDNECK

What's wrong with being a redneck?
Not everyone can fit the bill.
Although many keep trying,
There's so much to learn, still.

Imagine a world full of rednecks,
And how peaceful life would be.
There'd be no drive-by shootings,
Or burnings for people to see.

Redneck children are disciplined,
By fathers they dearly love.
There's nothing wrong with a spanking,
When your hand is guided from above.

Redneck women are beautiful,
They love and fight for their men.
They clean their houses and party,
Leaving them no time to sin.

Rednecks love to go racing, and
They can hunt and fish with the best.
While the criminal is up to no good,
Rednecks are getting some rest.

Rednecks will defend this nation,
As they love it and always will.
And a full-blooded American redneck
Never sleeps with his best friend-Bill.

THE VOLUNTEER

What does it take to be a volunteer?
I'm sure it can't be the money.
They must be poured from special molds,
As they work on rainy days or sunny.

Volunteers are needed at every level,
And I think I can name a few.
There's not too many who can take their place,
Or do the things they do.

A Red Cross worker can draw your blood,
Or will be there when disaster nears.
Firefighters respond 24 hours a day,
And will help us when fire appears.

Our teachers rely on the volunteer worker,
To assist our children with needs.
The Coast Guard Auxiliary is always ready,
Giving assistance at record speed.

SCORE will help with business plans,
If that's the direction you're going.
A Right to Life worker will offer you help,
Long before or after you're showing.

We should thank God for the volunteer,
They do it for the love of mankind.
Many deserve, but few receive,
True thanks, for the way they shine.

THE SENATOR

A senator's life is ever so lonely,
If the spouse is left at home.
Once they finish their busy day,
Both are totally alone.

Washington is a cruel place to live,
To those not wise to the ways.
It'll eat you up and spit you out,
And make you hate your days.

Dare I say some found a way,
To get through the lonely nights.
And many discovered over the years,
To make it, you learn how to fight.

Money being the root of all evil
Can easily lead one to him.
Once they sell our trust in them
Other types of evil creeps in.

Do politicians still work for the people?
Do lobbyists still work the halls?
Does greed and corruption still rule the day,
If so, our country will fall?

We, the people, sit back and wonder,
How officials lose their sight.
What's so difficult about going to work,
And doing what they know is right?

FOOTBALL HERO

To make it to the big league
I practiced all the time.
When they finally saw my talents
On Sunday, the game was mine.

I'm a simple football hero,
People love to see me run.
I work hard for my money,
Being paid for having fun.

The girls tried to woo me,
Before I played each game.
I knew what they were after
They couldn't pronounce my name.

The name is Rzeaumanenski.
It's a beautiful name to me.
When you can run and play like I do,
It's you they come out to see.

Never thought about being a hero,
I just love playing football.
Mama told me to get an education
Or I'd never play at all.

Now I'm just a football hero,
Who loves to play the game.
If you want to see me play,
Come out and shout my name.

MY SISTER

Only my sister knows how I feel,
Since she never leaves me alone.
She had me in bed by nine o'clock,
When mom and dad weren't home.

It was she who always tied my shoes,
And sent me off to school.
She always found the good in people,
And lived by the golden rule.

My sister deserved what life could give;
She was always good to me.
One day, God called her home,
An angel she'll always be.

If every kid had a sister like her
They'd be happy all the time.
Thank God for all she did,
My sister was one of a kind.

OUT ON THE TOWN

Woke up this morning,
Took the curlers from my hair.
And I washed this body
From my head to way down there.

Put some mascara on my eyes
A little rouge on my face.
Wore my very best garments
Made of shear black lace.

I started making plans
To take you out with me.
We're going to put on a show
For the whole town to see.

'Cause I'm going out on the town
With my very best friend.
Just want to have some fun
With a very sexy man.

Yes, the week was hot and heavy
I worked my fingers to the bone.
I earned a great weekend
And refuse to be alone.

We're going to dance the night away.
We'll have a drink or two.
Everything'll be fine
As long as I wake up next to you.

'Cause I'm going out on the town
With my very best friend.
Just want to have some fun
With a very sexy man.

We're going to dance the night away.
We'll have a drink or two.
Everything'll be fine
As long as I wake up next to you.

THAT LOOK OF YOURS

It's all about that look of yours,
That really gets to me.
Oh, how I'd love to step inside
To see the things you see.

God gave men and women eyes,
And we see things just the same.
Why you can't see what's clear to me,
Is driving me insane.

Take some time to think it over,
What's the reason that you cry?
Show me that smile, it'll be alright,
And you'll see it by and by.

As time goes by, life gets harder,
For us to try and work things out.
If we start right now, we can make it work,
With that, there's never a doubt.

Surely, you've seen Mona Lisa's smile,
That's puzzled us for years.
That look of hers is all it takes,
To drive a man to tears.

Take a little time to think it over.
Is there a reason for you to cry?
Show me that smile, it'll be alright,
And you'll see it by and by.

OLD FRIEND

I thought of an old friend of mine,
Just the other day.
Can't remember how long it's been,
Since they moved away.

I know we did some crazy things,
But can't remember why.
We tried to ride a sow one day,
And she threw us into a stye.

When it's left up to two young boys,
Trouble will find a way.
What starts off as childish fun,
Can easily ruin your day.

Bang! Bang! and some Shoot 'Em Up,
Games we played back then.
A shack with some windows we broke,
Came close to doing us in.

Our parents didn't take to kindly then,
To the damages, they had to pay.
But I'll never forget the fun we had,
That's lasted all these days.

Of all the people we meet each day,
A few stand out from the rest.
And over the years, you continue to prove
That my old friend was one of the best.

CAROLINA BLUE

It was never about the way you looked,
Or the way you fixed your hair.
It was never about the way you walked,
That showed your natural flair.

It was never about the way you dressed,
Or the way you showed your style.
It was never about the way you glowed,
Or that Mona Lisa smile.

It was never about your sexy voice,
Or the things you chose to wear.
It was never about your tender touch,
Or that special trait you share.

It was always about your eyes of blue,
That always appealed to me.
Can't get enough of those blue eyes,
That God gave you to see.

If you didn't have those piercing eyes,
You'd be like all the rest.
For me, it was always your eyes of blue.
That made you look your best.

Then I think it was all those things,
That attracted me to you.
But the most important thing of all,
Were your eyes of Carolina blue.

ONE MORE CHANCE

I'm trying to resolve a problem,
That's been troubling me today.
If you plan to kick me out,
Then where am I going to stay?

Will you give me one more chance,
And forgive me, won't you please?
Today, I'll give my solemn word,
Let me put your mind at ease.

Over the years, we've done a lot,
To the house I built for you.
So why do you want to tear it apart,
By doing what you plan to do?

Come on, girl, and give me a chance,
And forgive me, won't you please?
Today, you'll get my solemn word,
That'll put your mind at ease.

I can't deny the words I've said,
Or the things I did to you.
But was it enough to end it all?
I pray that we're not through.

Open wide your heart today!
We should talk, so please don't run.
I've been wanting to tell you again
That you're my only one.

So, give me one more chance, my dear,
And forgive me, won't you please?
Today, I'll pledge my love to you,
If it'll put your mind at ease.

WHAT ABOUT THE CHILDREN

Two people met and fell in love
But they were not the same race.
True love doesn't know color,
It grows when given the space.

"But what about the children?" I asked.
"Why force them to make a choice?"
"Does anyone care what the child would say,
Then who's going to be their voice?"

If two young people are left alone,
But can't control their passion.
In the blink of an eye, a child is conceived,
Now, she wants an abortion.

"But what about the children?" I asked.
They'll be forced to make a choice.
"Does anyone care what the child would say,
Then who's going to be their voice?"

Some parents today are too selfish,
Being more concerned about things.
All they think about is themselves,
Fine jewelry, necklaces, and rings.

"But what about the children?" I asked.
"And what would be their choice?"
"If the parents want to kill them,
The state should be their voice."

I CHOSE YOU

Considering the girls in town that day, I chose you.
Of all the women I could have married, I chose you.
I chose you for your beautiful smile.
I chose you because you were good, not wild.

I chose you for accepting my style, I chose you.
You never took advantage of me, so I chose you.
You never played me for a fool, so I chose you.
I chose you for what I saw in you.

I chose you because you believed in me, too.
I chose you for the love and things you do, I chose you.
You never teased me with your charm, so I chose you.
You never tried to ignore my love, so I chose you.

I chose you for your beauty and grace.
I chose you for the smile on your face.
I chose you for keeping up with me, I chose you.
You always took me one day at a time, so I chose you.

You were so sweet when you talked to me, so I chose you.
I chose you because I love you so.
I chose you this time and will never let go,
And if I had it to do over again, I'd still choose you.

I LOVE YOU

It bothers me deeply that I brought you pain,
Physical or emotional; it's all the same.
The words I said made sense at the time,
But now I see how they can trick a mind.

The woman I love has a heart so pure,
Never a problem we couldn't endure.
My chance at love was taken away,
I long for her voice at the end of the day.

My love runs deep and touches her soul,
Love doesn't matter if you're young or old.
The love I have, grows stronger by the day,
And it shouldn't be long before I hear her say.

"I love you dearly with all my heart,
I'll let go of the past as we make a new start.
All I ask, is that you love me as much,
As in years past, before we lost touch."

The times we had, God filled us with love.
I truly think we were blessed from above.
If you take a chance, I'll promise you this:
We'll end each day with a soft, gentle kiss.

Now's your chance, as I've had my say.
Please I beg of you, don't send me away.
Take a chance on me, and I'll prove my love,
It'll be as good as you've always dreamed of.

STARTING OVER

Starting over is so hard to do,
As memories are slowly erased.
But when it's time to let it go,
Run fast like a man being chased.

Some people think of the sin,
That changes what God joined together.
But consider the sin of living a lie,
And hating the day that you met her.

Untie my hands and set me free,
Let's correct the mess we've made.
With time, all pain will go away
And we'll forget the plans we laid.

Marriages work best when shared by two,
And dissolves if one goes astray.
They also thrive on love and respect,
That's renewed with each passing day.

Think long and hard of the children,
Do they deserve the pain and tears?
Save the love that you have left,
And share it throughout the years.

Starting over is so hard to do,
As memories are slowly erased.
But when it's time to let it go,
Run fast like a man being chased.

BRIDGES

The bridges we burned long, long ago,
Are being rebuilt today.
After living a life of misery and guilt,
I think I can honestly say.

Of all the women I've known before,
You're the only one for me.
If you'll allow me back in your life,
Faithful, I promise to be.

Let's mend the bridges we burned back then,
And start our lives anew.
I hope you'll agree to give us a try,
If not, I'll bid you ado.

I was told to pack, to leave our house,
And to get out of your life.
And never again, for as long as I live,
Will I ever call you my wife.

It's been thirty years since we parted,
But now we're together again.
I love that silvery gray hair of yours,
I beg you to take me in.

Let's mend those bridges one by one,
And start our life anew.
If you'll just agree to love me again,
I'll give my love to you.

THE RAMBLING MAN

"Are you leaving me again?" I asked.
Well, this time, it'll be just fine.
You might as well go far away,
As you were never really mine.

You played me for a fool again,
I knew you were messing around.
At first, I wanted to buy you a ring,
But that wouldn't settle you down.

Don't ever try those tricks on me,
Cause I've had my final say.
You've tried pulling my strings before
But it won't happen today.

I gave you all my loving,
And I pledged my life to you.
Then I prayed to God almighty.
To help us see it through.

As a river never stops flowing
On its slow trip down to the sea.
There's a rambling man inside of me,
That'll be what it was meant to be.

A CHANGE OF HEART

I met her on a clear afternoon,
While jogging through the park.
I knew this was the girl for me,
And we talked well past dark.

Our lives were joined by marriage,
The love was there from the start.
Then, a very strange thing happened,
She was having a change of heart.

I have no idea what caused it,
Or where our love went wrong.
I put you on a pedestal,
I placed you on a throne.

Then you stopped saying I love you.
Did you ever really care?
I don't like the change I'm seeing,
I don't like what's in the air.

Is there something you want to tell me?
Is there something that I should know?
Is there a chance this marriage is over?
Or are you doing this just for show?

Along the way, you betrayed my trust.
Why was I played for such a fool?
Your words were always beautiful,
So how'd you end up this cruel?

If I could live this life over,
I'd have to live it the same.
It was you who failed our marriage.
And you'll never wear my name.

BELLE

I'll be sleeping on the prairie tonight,
Just my old horse Charlie and me.
I left my Belle back East one day,
And it's she that I long to see.

I'm on my way to California,
And it's a fortune that I seek.
Gold was found by a mill one day,
And it still hasn't reached its peak.

I told my Belle she could follow me,
When my sacks were full of gold.
That I would take good care of her,
Before my bones got too old.

I dodged some arrows the Indians shot,
As they didn't like us that much.
I always tried to stay hidden away
In the thickets, thorns, and such.

Well, I've been here for a year or so,
And saved a very large stake.
Now, I can send for my sweet girl Belle,
Or would that be a mistake?

A visiting friend done told me,
That my Belle was never at home.
She went and took a dancing job,
And my Belle was never alone.

THROW ME A LINE

"Come on and throw me a line," I said.
"Cause you're sinking awfully fast."
If you plan to get there with me
Try throwing me one that'll last.

I've heard every line in the book, I think.
And frankly, yours are old.
If you want my heart to skip and flutter,
Try saying something new and bold.

Finally, he had settled down a bit,
So I decided to ask for his name.
"What brings you to our little town, I asked.
And I thank you, just the same."

Why do you think men act that way,
When looking for a woman they adore?
Why can't they just be themselves,
And say the right words for sure?

I can honestly say that I love you,
If I can ever be so bold.
Let's sit over there by the window,
And I'll order us something cold.

We've enjoyed many hours together:
We ate, we talked, we danced.
Then I thanked him for throwing the line,
That led to this beautiful romance.

AN UNGODLY MAN

When you came looking for me,
Your head was hanging low.
You told me you were leaving him,
But had no place to go.

The man of your dreams
Had lost his charm.
And you did what you could,
To hide the bruises on your arm.

If your marriage isn't working,
You have to take a stand.
Because you never waste your life
On an ungodly man.

It's never been that easy
To tell you what to do.
But no one truly deserves,
What this man has done to you.

There's no room for bitterness,
In a marriage of today.
But when there's love and respect,
Then, neither one should stray.

I share with you this message,
It takes two to make a home.
But if you fail to do your part,
You'll end up on your own.

THE DOOR

Well, you put me down again, girl,
But don't ever count me out.
You know it's not my first time,
And with that, there's never a doubt.

It took some time to work it out,
But thanks to you, I'll run.
You love to throw your fiery darts,
It's your way of having fun.

But fun like yours is a terrible thing,
And it hurts people for sure.
The more you do those nasty things,
The closer I walk to the door.

Doors are just a portal to life,
That can open wide, or close.
Pay attention to what's going on,
And pick the right time to dose.

I had to take some time off work,
To make a suitable plan.
I was never the one to give up,
But I'll never be your man.

You put me down for the very last time,
Now, I'll show you a thing or two.
When you get home from work tonight
The only one there will be you.

IN MY SHOES

You can stop the world tonight,
It's time to call it a day.
Sure, I wanted to be with you,
But I couldn't find a way.

I tend to lose a little control,
The longer I stay with you.
I can never see a life for us,
Unless you're faithful and true.

I haven't seen a change in you,
Since the day we said goodbye.
You would always talk about him,
As you looked me in the eye.

Wouldn't you like to settle down?
Are you happy with another?
Do you really like being single,
Never to be a mother?

If you put yourself in my shoes,
And recall the things I've said.
Your heart and mind would tell you,
The reasons I left your bed.

Now that you have your freedom,
You can do just as you please.
The best I can say is thank you,
For putting my mind at ease.

I'VE GOT TROUBLES

Troubles have a way of finding us,
And you know that anything goes.
Some are worse off than others,
Like those without fingers or toes.

Do I have troubles, you may ask?
"I do, like never before."
You better believe I have them,
And more are knocking at the door.

Even the children have troubles, I say,
Cause troubles are all over schools.
I had my own set of troubles then,
And the teacher sat me on a stool.

All the troubles I've had in life,
Have followed me around the world.
Talk about troubles that make you cry,
Man, I never found the right girl.

For what it's worth, I still have troubles,
I don't even have a home.
With troubles like mine, you can't settle down,
It's not easy being alone.

There's no escaping life's troubles,
As they're with us every day.
If your troubles show their ugly head,
They'll test you and won't go away.

THE GOOD TIMES

As I lay here on my sofa,
You're sitting back in your chair.
I'm reading the latest gossip,
While you fiddle with thinning hair.

You've been here for a little while.
I saw you coming through the door.
We kissed, and you said you loved me.
That was it, as I longed for more.

Can't you talk to me a little,
And tell me about your day?
You've been gone for ten long hours,
So, you should have a lot to say.

I remember all the good times,
We were young and looking around.
We were both seeking attention,
Where romance and sweet love abound.

Add a little more conversation,
I'd be as happy as I could be.
Combine some love and affection!
There's so much more you'll see.

But now it seems you've given up,
Or you've slipped into a trance.
I wonder why you're leaving me,
Didn't I give you enough romance?

TWO OF A KIND

I feel the start of a new life,
As my old one ended with you.
Let's continue the path we're on,
There's nothing we can't do.

No one has gotten this close to me,
But you found a way to my heart.
Now, I look forward to each new day,
As I hope for a brand-new start.

You broke the ice when you said, "Hello."
My life has purpose, I know who I am.
I don't understand what you saw in me,
But I'm glad to be your man.

Until I met you, life had no meaning.
I had no direction, no place to go.
You changed a man; you changed his life.
You wanted to marry; I made it so.

And now we're two of a kind,
As both have a purpose in life.
You took a man who had no hope,
Who now, has you as his wife.

THE WHISPER

W hisper the words I long to hear,
Whisper them soft and low.
Whisper the words that give me joy,
As our love continues to grow.

Two people found each other.
Over time, they fell in love.
They worked hard to keep it together
And will try to live as the dove.

Possessions can bring you happiness,
Or you could marry one of a kind.
But if love isn't part of the equation,
You'll never have peace of mind.

Always consider the needs of others
In the things you say and do.
When the sun sets over mountains high,
Your friends will be there for you.

During the time you have together,
Continue to rid her of fear.
As you snuggle, she'll melt in your arms,
As you whisper what she longs to hear.

THE SECRET

Two people got married,
They vowed, "till death do us part."
So, why are there so many divorces,
Before they have a chance to start?

Take your vows more seriously,
Not forgetting, as time goes by.
Love, honor, and cherish your spouse,
And continue till the day you die.

Once married, your life will change,
Now you have a partner for life.
Start thinking more of each other,
And never forget your wife.

I'm told the purpose of a courtship
Is to get your problems resolved.
Tears fall when a marriage breaks up,
Especially if kids are involved.

The preacher changed your single life,
Not one, but now there's two.
If each precious day is remembered,
We can prevent a fight with you.

The secret to having a good marriage,
Is found in the pages of a book.
So, take your Bible off the shelf.
There's help everywhere you look.

CRY A TEAR

She married me in ole Mexico,
On a warm and sunny day.
She liked being around people,
And enjoyed the children at play.

We explored the land and ate the food,
As we learned to love them all.
We had to leave as the time drew near,
Which started our downfall.

She looked around to find her a place,
Taking minutes, days, and hours.
I bought the house she'd dreamed of
And we tried to make it ours.

Won't you cry a tear for me today
As I've lost my one true love?
She had to adjust to married life
But only needed a shove.

Her heart was good, and purpose-driven,
But she couldn't make the change.
We talked of things we had to do,
The easy ones and the long-range.

Her love of the land was calling her back,
And she asked me to go with her.
My life was set, my roots ran deep,
And staying at home was preferred.

Won't you cry a tear for me? I prayed
As I've lost my one true love.
She couldn't adjust to married life,
And decided to let go of.

LET'S SNUGGLE AWHILE

I praise the day he gave you away,
By walking out the door on you.
I truly believe he lost his mind,
When he said that, he was through.

There's nothing better on days like these,
Than, being with the one you adore.
There are so many things that we can do,
Knowing what's truly in store.

We can sit by the lake, catch up on life,
Or sit quietly while holding hands.
We can lay on the shore side by side,
As our lives make no demands.

Later, we'll take a ride in the country,
Or sit by the river's edge.
It doesn't matter where the road ends,
My love is forever, I pledge.

I can visit you at your house today,
Or you can do the same at mine.
We can come and go just as we please,
All the while, we're towing the line.

Come on down, let's snuggle awhile,
We'll see where it leads from there.
It surely beats staying at home,
On your porch in an old rocking chair.

THE FEVER

It's been well over a year,
Since you walked out the door.
The house is quiet and lonely,
Sort of like it was before.

The day was bright and cheerful,
With children playing all around.
I think I've cried a million tears
Since the day you left our town.

The one thing that brings me peace,
Is to think back over time.
The good things I stored away
Have always cleared my mind.

One day, when the fever leaves,
I hope you'll remember me.
Maybe then, if it's not too late,
We can stand where all can see.

The flames burn deep in my heart,
And will never be put out.
"The magic we had will last forever!"
Those words I will gladly shout.

So don't you take forever,
'Cause I'm not a patient man.
If you think we have a chance,
I'll do everything I can.

THE TRUCK DRIVER

I've been driving way too long,
And the love is fading away.
I've been gone for a very long time,
Going home this time to stay.

I took this job to see our country,
And never got tired of the sights.
Every time I drove the backroads,
I regretted the lonely nights.

I drove a truck for many years,
And won't forget what I've seen.
Now that it was about to end,
My replacement was oh-so green.

I parked my rig, my job was finished,
Now, sleep was the order of the day.
I called my wife and headed east,
And the skies were cloudy and gray.

I saw the signs welcoming me home,
Man, were they good to see.
I saw her standing there on the porch,
So happy I could see her glee.

Finally, we'd live as man and wife,
And do the things we'd dreamed.
Never to roam the country again
So happy, she wanted to scream.

A LOVE STORY

I think we were destined to be,
At a time, we knew not when.
Although we were tied to others,
Two lives were bound to end.

My true love was wed to another,
In whose eyes she couldn't do right.
He seemed to keep her tied to a string,
As he pushed for another fight.

I returned home one cool evening,
My wife was in bed with another.
We'd been one in the eyes of God,
But now, it would go no further.

Chance brought us back together,
And nothing will tear us apart.
I lost my wife to another man,
Who wasn't right from the start.

Our old lives kept us apart,
And the new ones brought us here.
We're on the verge of doing things right,
As our future was never this clear.

The two of us are older now,
What a blessing it had to be.
Brought together by the grace of God,
Not afraid of what others perceive.

TALKING ABOUT LONELY

I've spent my nights and days as well,
Preparing since way back then.
All through school, I was looking for you,
Can't imagine doing that again.

It's Friday night, and I'm out on the town,
Still looking for a man like you.
I've wandered around from place to place,
Not finding one that'll do.

If you're talking about being lonely,
I'm as lonely as I can be.
If you're talking about being in love,
There's no one but you for me.

If you're out looking for a man,
Some courage will always do.
What I want from a man is respect,
And for him to love me true.

Well, I've been out here for a while,
Still looking for a man to love.
I've wandered around from place to place,
Looking here, there, and above.

I know God wouldn't plan it this way,
Two people alone each night.
So why not invite me in for a drink
We'll start our lives off right.

How can a woman choose to live,
Without the love of a good-hearted man.
As all good men are a gift from God
To love as only we can.

So never in this life, do I ever plan
To be that lonely again.
And now that we're finally together,
We're there, till God knows when.

A CHANCE MEETING

Two teens, by chance, met one day,
And their love began to grow.
Whatever they had, they shared together,
And their faces gave off a glow.

At school, they were always together,
And he gave up sports for her.
They talked, and talked, of future plans,
And their passions began to stir.

Two young kids, thrown together,
Choose one to date the other.
Always seen as they drove through town,
In a truck owned by his brother.

One bright afternoon, they argued,
Over what, we'd never know.
He left early from school one day,
Confused, with nowhere to go.

He was seen driving around town,
And his truck was found the next day.
For whatever reason, he took his life
Never to see her again.

At school one day, she heard the news
And her whole life looked grim.
Later found lying next to a gun,
She was determined to be with him.

They were two of God's little children,
And now they'll have to face Him.
Whatever provoked their deadly act,
Their futures with God looked dim.

THE SLAMMING DOOR

I returned home one night;
I saw a note on the floor.
I looked around the house,
I heard the slamming door.

Leaving was no surprise;
I'll go on without you.
I saw that you were gone.
I didn't know what to do.

I loved you from the start.
I never wanted you to go.
I hated the way it ended.
I truly loved you so.

You were always steadfast,
From morning to setting sun.
I kept begging you to stay,
But your persistence won.

Thinking back, I can recall
The sound of the slamming door.
Cruel is the way you left me.
I cried, lying on the floor.

Your kisses had no passion.
Your love, I didn't know.
You were like a stranger.
Good riddance, now please go.

A NIGHT ON THE TOWN

I promised myself a night on the town
To search for a girl for me.
I've wandered around from place to place,
Never knowing which one it would be.

My standards are high, she'll believe in God.
Not any young lady will do.
My heart tells me she's out there
And my thoughts are always on you.

Most men need a woman to love,
And I'm sure they'll want romance.
Men and women must procreate
If the world is to have a chance.

How can a man live in this world
Without the love of a girl?
We take our women usually for life
To try and show them the world.

I've been thinking of the one I'll find.
And the words I'll need to say.
I know you're out there somewhere.
I believe we'll meet someday.

Unbeknownst to me, my troubles would end,
On a beautiful day like this.
I got her attention with the word – hello!
And the rest was Heavenly bliss.

CRUISING THE STREETS

I'm cruising the streets on a Saturday night,
Searching for a girl, that's true.
Wandering around from place to place,
Not finding a girl that'll do.

I always worked long days and nights,
Preparing since I was a teen.
I know in my heart you must be there,
And my thoughts are always serene.

People, I think, need someone to love,
For companionship and romance.
And that's the way our life should be,
If love is to have a chance.

How can anyone go through life,
Without the love of a girl?
And God gave Adam a woman,
So, they could fill the world.

Where can I go to meet you,
And will I ever know what to say?
Why do things move this slow,
And why are we made this way?

A friend and I were standing at a bar,
As we checked the happening scene.
I told the waiter to bring us a drink,
And I told her my name was Eugene.

I REMEMBER

I came to Carolina
To reminisce and ease my mind.
I planned to see the old haunts
That were not lost to time.

I was walking down the boardwalk
When my thoughts turned back to you.
As I recalled the fun and good times
That we had in '62.

I remember buying donuts
Down at Britt's Donut Shop.
I remember bars and dance halls
Where the kids danced the Bop.

I remember body surfing then,
When the waves made their run.
And skimming o'er the sand.
Finding ways to have some fun.

I remember seeing you out there,
Talking to one of your friends.
And I knew right then you'd be my girl
Before the summer ends.

We found the time to slip away.
We found the time to dance.
But an old flame came back to you
And destroyed our budding romance.

ALL THESE TEARS

I brushed my teeth and washed my face.
Then dried my hands 'fore saying grace.
I can't believe that we're through
I gave my love and my life to you.

We had some good years and some bad.
While making do with what we had.
I cared for you, you cared for me,
We were so content to let it be.

So, why'd you leave me? Where'd you go?
And are you close now, I don't know?
You took from me, my very best years.
And left me here, with all these tears.

You were my love; you were my life.
You wanted a friend; I wanted a wife.
So, where'd I go wrong, what'd I miss?
Never thought, it would end like this.

So, why'd you leave me? Where'd you go?
And are you close now, I don't know?
You took from me, my best years
And left me here, with all these tears.

I used to think our love was good,
But as we aged, I understood.
And in this house, we both called home,
Is where I now stay all alone.

So, why'd you leave me? Where'd you go?
And are you close now, I don't know?
You took from me, my very best years
And left me here, with all these tears.

We had some good years and some bad.
While making do with what we had.
I cared for you, you cared for me
We were content, to let it be.

In this house that was built for two
You loved me, and I loved you.
It was meant to last, 'til our old age.
But you took us, to a different stage.

THE RIPPLE

A ripple forms on the ocean top,
Born from a quake far below.
As it begins to move o'er the water,
The ripple begins to grow.

There on an island shine the rays of the sun,
As the villagers go about their day.
A carefree people with not a worry one,
Has a visitor coming their way.

Out on the ocean, the waves are calm,
No sign of the trouble that's brewing.
Back on the mainland, the machines reveal,
The tranquility will soon become ruin.

A decision was made to sound the alarm,
As it traveled for thousands of miles.
The villagers finally got a look
And it quickly erased their smiles.

There on the island where the kids play,
The people were oblivious to all.
The ripple drew closer as the hours passed,
Was measured at forty feet tall.

The small ripple had grown after all,
And with a devastating force, it struck.
The peaceful village where so many lived,
Had finally run out of luck.

PLANE DOWN

It was a typical sunny morning,
As I think back and recall.
Things would change by day's end
And we'd all feel ten feet tall.

The alarm rang, we flew to the site,
Where a plane had just gone down.
A crewman spotted the wreckage,
After hours of looking around.

He saw a glitter of the sun's light,
On the wreckage far below.
Two of us were hoisted down,
Their status, we did not know.

A biplane had crashed that day,
With its nose pointed down.
The pilot died on contact,
When the plane struck the ground.

We continued to look around,
After hearing a faint yell.
His passenger was bent forward,
On the stick, he was impaled.

Soon after cutting him lose,
The rescue was underway.
We hoisted him up to the chopper,
He'd live for another day.

THE END OF THE ROAD

The open road at one in the morning
Is a lonely place to be.
All there is, is you and the road,
And, of course, the ole CB.

Your wife and kids were left behind,
But at least they're safe at home.
If it were not for the voices in the night,
You'd be out there alone.

But driving a rig is the job you chose,
And it's a noble profession at that.
These kings of the road deliver our goods,
And deserve a tip of the hat.

To do their jobs, they sacrifice all,
And the rigs continue to run.
They drive through storms, blizzards, and such,
While I'm out having some fun.

With a deadline to meet, they drive all night,
As the load must be there by dawn.
Suddenly, a car darts out in front.
And you're forced to lay on the horn.

After hitting your brakes, God smiles at you,
And you're able to deliver your load.
After you sleep, you head back home,
With your family at the end of the road.

BLACK CLOUD RISING

I once had a wife and family,
And a very nice place to stay.
I had a job and a very fast car,
And a church where I went to pray.

Everyone needs a good wife,
Like the one God gave to me.
I like to think that all my friends,
Are as happy as they can be.

I grew up young and handsome.
I had plans, wants, and needs.
My college life was so much fun,
I was always expected to lead.

But then my whole life changed,
As it took a turn for the worse.
Hate and anger slowly crept in,
It was like I'd been cursed.

There's a black cloud rising,
Somewhere over my head.
It wasn't hard to see it forming,
As the skies were dark and red.

There's no way that I can stop it,
And life is not always fair.
Mine, like yours, has its ups and downs,
And my fate was up in the air.

A JOURNEY THROUGH SPACE

I've reached the edge of the solar system,
And took a look back toward earth.
I've always wondered what lies out there,
Since a few years after my birth.

I volunteered many years ago,
And my supplies were stored on this ship.
I've been rocketing to God knows where,
Since giving Earth's gravity the slip.

I've already seen the rings of Saturn,
And the rest of the planets but one.
I've seen the stars as they passed me by,
And came face to face with the sun.

I've seen the wonders of the universe,
Comets, meteors, and things.
I can't imagine what awaits me out there,
As I record everything that it brings.

This trip I'm on will be one-way,
New adventures, black holes, and pillars of light.
Oh! What a mystery they are to me,
Many different shapes, and the colors are bright.

I take this trip gladly,
And will see what our scopes never caught.
History will record when I leave the earth,
And I hope to find what man has sought.

THE GROOVE

I've worked all day - I'm as tired as can be,
And I'm taking this old body home.
But the woman I married many years ago,
Refuses to leave me alone.

When I'm at home, she's on my back,
With trivial things to do.
When I think back to our wedding day,
We planned a great life for two.

I don't know what happened to us,
Don't know who made the wrong move.
I thought we had many years left,
And we were still in the groove.

I lost my hair, my teeth are gone,
And I've gained a pound or two.
But that won't stop us from doing things,
That married couples do.

Doesn't matter that you weigh a ton,
And you have enough skin for two.
What I miss is the woman I married,
Whose love was all I knew.

Put aside the fact that we're old and worn,
And you'll start to see things move.
Then imagine all the fun we've had,
When we were very much in the groove.

THERE HAD TO BE MORE

I walked to the edge of the river,
And looked to the other shore.
I never knew what awaited me there,
But man, there had to be more.

Grew up poor in a dusty old town,
With a saloon and general store.
It was never much to brag about;
I knew there had to be more.

The people in town looked down on us,
We were blessed but very poor.
Try as we did, life beat us back down,
So, man, there had to be more.

There has to be more on the West side,
Over here, there's nothing for me.
On the distant shore of the river
Is the place I longed to be.

I considered a few options,
Feeling bad down to the core.
My hometown still had nothing,
So, man, there has to be more.

My bag was packed, and school was over,
So I walked to my front door.
I have to see what awaits me there,
Cause, man, there had to be more.

So, I crossed that river and headed West
Keeping the word, that I swore.
That I'd leave home and start a new life
'Cause, man, there had to be more.

And what I found on the other side
Is what I'd been looking for.
So very glad that I made it there,
For me, there was definitely more.

SUGAR DADDY

I never had luck with a girl like you,
But I gave it a try or two.
The thought of it never entered my mind,
Until the day that I met you.

Wife number one was a fine old lady,
But she couldn't cook a thing.
She loved herself more than I ever could,
I was forced to remove my ring.

As luck would have it, I tried it again,
And made her wife number two.
She told me later she didn't clean house.
What's a man supposed to do?

I gave her up and wandered about,
Being sick of all the strife.
It seemed to work; I didn't have a care,
Until she entered my life.

I loved that sparkle in her eyes,
And her heart was pure as gold.
A vow I made that never again,
As the last two made me old.

So let me be your Sugar Daddy,
I'll take good care of you.
Just let me be your Sugar Daddy.
I'll do what you want me to.

Sugar daddies are the kind of men,
That every woman will need.
Sugar daddies never make demands,
Their only job is to please.

APPLY WITHIN

I rode into town on my horse named Fred,
Much like I'd done before.
The day was hot, and the land was parched,
And my backside was damp and soar.

I'd been on the trail for a day or so,
Still looking for work that was good.
I thought I'd found it in the local saloon,
But apparently, I misunderstood.

The sign read — Wanted: Apply Within,
Someone to manage my crew.
Thought I'd found a good steady job,
Then, I learned what the ladies do.

A foreman saw me standing by the bar,
And asked me if I'd like to punch cows.
It sounded okay, so I said, "Why not?"
And he said, "We'd have to leave now."

We got to the ranch, he showed me around,
And told me where to stow my gear.
I'd been on the job for a day or two,
He asked, "What did you do to my steers."

Well, "I punched them once, and I punched them twice,
And they fell to the ground quite dead."
I heard him shouting and the sound of his gun,
As I raced back to town on Fred.

MY CHIMP AND I

I walk with a limp, and I have a chimp,
That loves to rub my face.
I didn't pay much, so I'll keep him around,
And I can't take him any place.

He's such a wimp, that crazy little chimp,
When out, his mouth is held wide.
Walking the crowd, he looks for a morsel,
And his shame, he takes in stride.

The little fellow flirts with the girls,
He knows how to draw a crowd.
My chimp and I go from town to town,
I train him, so he's not that loud.

As I'm talking, he walks around,
With an eye on something good.
He picks a lady and brings her over,
All the rest is understood.

Standing there, he points to his mouth,
As he waits for something to eat.
With the system I use, we help each other,
While grinning, he then takes his seat.

Over the years, I taught him a lot,
He can sign and has lots to say.
My old friend tells me time and again,
Won't you send me home one day.

THE MEDICINE MAN

The noonday sun was glaring hot,
And the crowds were gathering 'round.
Families and friends had waited all week,
The medicine man was back in town.

His weathered face and scarred hands
Gave clues to his troubled past.
The old ways were slowly waning,
As nothing is meant to last.

The sounds of his drum and snakes' rattle
Kept the beat of his native dance.
How noble he looked in his buckskin clothes,
His headdress, tomahawk, and lance.

His age was a testament to what he knew,
About the plants, the earth, and sky.
The people were amazed at the show he gave,
And the kids never closed an eye.

He hocked his wares when the show was over:
The ointments, liniments, and herbs.
The things he carried were for man or beast,
That cured them, horses, and herds.

The time had come for him to move on;
Another town was around the bend.
How many shows were yet to come,
Before his time would come to an end?

The days of the medicine show were over,
As towns let go of the past.
He'd performed many wondrous shows,
But this one would be his last.

THE MEXICAN

The Mexican broke out of jail,
And quickly rode off to El Paso.
There, he'd find a sweet little woman,
Who went by the name of Calico.

As he grew, he got mean and tough,
And was feared all along the border.
But little did he know that one day soon,
A woman would give his life order.

The Mexican was skilled with a horse and gun,
And could ride and shoot with the best.
But he knew somewhere deep inside,
He could soon be laid to rest.

The Mexican was tired as he rode into town,
And his eyes kept moving about.
Kept looking for trouble and a place to stay,
When he heard a sweet lady shout.

Off to the side were several cowboys,
Who were trying to mess with her.
But as he approached to break things up,
They ran off without a stir.

Calico was known to be smart and witty,
And easily saw through the grime.
Something great was about to happen,
As they both had nothing but time.

THE NATIVE AMERICAN

I want to tell you a story,
That hasn't been told before.
It started here in this country,
Back in the days of yore.

As we spread all over the country,
We fought and settled the land.
We eventually forced the natives out,
Despite their noble stand.

We took away their hunting grounds,
And killed those we despised.
We pushed them out without regret,
They were savages and uncivilized.

Under the guise of eminent domain,
Our government made the rules.
People moved in and built the towns,
With stores, churches, and schools.

From many tribes, these people came,
And on reservations, they stayed.
No longer allowed to hunt the land,
Their numbers continued to fade.

They were a proud and noble people,
Representing different bands.
Today, they're known as Native Americans
But they came from far-off lands.

REBECCA

W hen the tumbleweed rolls off the western plains,
It's always guided by the wind.
But when a drifter gets in the saddle,
He's driven by a marriage on the mend.

His darling Rebecca took their son,
And headed for a frontier town.
She said to Sam, "When you get out of jail,
Come west and track us down."

She purchased a wagon, horses, and food,
And joined a train going west.
She heard all about the free land there,
And decided she'd give it her best.

In Oklahoma, she left the train,
And searched 'till it caught her eye.
With a stake in the ground, she claimed the land,
A place to live, work, and die.

Sam was out and started his search,
But Rebecca, could not be found.
Five years passed, he was ready to quit,
When Rebecca came riding to town.

Now, they had a good home and more,
And didn't mind the work and toil.
As they slowly renewed their lives,
The ranchers kept pumping up oil.

THE AMERICAN COWBOY

I'm an American Cowboy
And I ride the open range.
I'm gone for many months on end,
Fence posts I'm sent to change.

When I return and clean things up,
I relax by going to town.
If you come looking for me,
The saloon is where I'm found.

A cowboy's life is rough and hard,
They work the steers by day.
For weeks on end, they search the fields,
For the ones that went astray.

The cowboy's life is oh so lonely,
Nice women are but a dream.
Hour after hour, they work the ranch,
For pay, they lose in a game.

Willie sang some cowboy songs,
As heroes, they were to him.
Marty sang of El Paso town,
And cowboys, tall and slim.

Kids of the day looked up to them.
Cowboys and Indians, they'd play.
White hats were worn by the good guys,
And they always saved the day.

HOPE

The hope we share will never fade,
'Till the death angel comes along.
And if we fail to maintain hope,
We'll lose out to the strong.

Hope will keep a smile on our face,
And the wrinkles from our brow.
Hope has a way of keeping us strong,
While working the here and now.

Hope keeps our children laughing,
As mothers watch over them.
Hope still brings people together,
And he's convinced that she's a gem.

If hope is seen as the fabric
That binds two hearts together.
Then love is the thread of life
That connects the two forever.

If hope begins to fade away
Two lives will drift apart.
Without something to hope for
Love ends with two shattered hearts.

If you find a way, love stays alive,
Through the morn' and all your day.
The love we've had these many years,
So strong and will never fade.

LOVES DESTINY—GRACE

Tell me again that you love me,
As I like to hear your voice.
You were always sweet and lovely,
So convinced I made a good choice.

Some marriages are a blessing,
But yours should never have been.
The man you chose was full of hate,
And I know I'm better than him.

Doctors worked to repair your face,
But the scars will never fade.
Then, one day, you allowed me in,
And I'm so glad you let me stay.

I knew the man you married,
And the things he did to you.
The love we share will always shine,
It'll prove what true love can do.

With you, my love, life is better,
Our love forever grows.
The way we met was magical,
As your life had stooped so low.

Despite the damage he caused you,
You're always beautiful to me.
Never ashamed to show the world,
What true love was meant to be.

SHARE THE MOMENT

The turkey's on the table,
And the family is coming home.
This won't be like years past,
When we both sat here alone.

The kids are making noises,
Much the same as we did then.
Family traditions keep us going,
And we hope they'll never end.

We bow our heads for the blessing,
The table is a sight to see.
All to be washed down slowly,
With some iced water, wine, or tea.

Later, we'll sit and talk awhile,
Or watch some football on TV.
We'll remember those we've lost,
All we'd still love to see.

If the world could share a moment,
With some talk and plenty to eat.
Famine erased from the face of the earth,
A stranger we'd never meet.

Today, we gave thanks for our blessings.
At Christmas, we'll give thanks to Him.
The holidays are now upon us,
And His spirit will never end.

SUMMER DREAMS

My summer dreams, are always with me,
And it seems they're here to stay.
Summer dreams, are always changing,
And it seems mine changed today.

Summer dreams, bring out the loving,
And it seems I love you now.
Summer dreams, will keep you smiling,
And it seems I've made a vow.

Summer is the time to make new friends.
Summer is the time to remember when.
Summer is the time you start new things.
Summer is the time you like to dream those Summer dreams.

Summer dreams, will cause a heartache,
And it seems mine aches for you.
Summer dreams, will start you crying,
And it seems I cry some, too.

Summer dreams, bring out the laughter,
And it seems I'm laughing now.
Summer dreams, are always ending,
And it seems I'll take my bow.

Summer is the time to make new friends.
Summer is the time to remember when.
Summer is the time you start new things.
Summer is the time you like to dream those, Summer dreams.

ME

C all me old-fashioned if you have to,
The games we played were tried and true.
We enjoyed the toys we got back then,
Some didn't make it, and some we'd mend.

The life of people changed back then,
And mothers cared for home and kin.
The menfolk had to work the farm,
And kept the family from sin and harm.

In today's world, things aren't the same.
Some girls won't change their name.
Children today are the victims of lust.
Keep an eye out for those you don't trust.

Busy mothers want sitters on call.
Lazy mothers go shopping at the mall.
Mothers today have no time for a book,
Some mothers were never taught to cook.

Messing around is on the rise today.
Cheating is old, but it's here to stay.
Some women chose to abort their child
Or deliver it just to let them run wild.

Like it or not, there's no place for "me."
If it's a family, you want to be.
Parents always provide for the home,
And children should never grow up alone.

THE STRUGGLE

I 've had to struggle all of my life,
But now I can stare it in the face.
I always tried to do things right,
And could never stand disgrace.

I always wore the right clothes to school
And my hair was ever so neat.
My parents taught me good manners,
And provided shoes for my feet.

Some kids decide to take their own lives,
And I'm required to clock in at work.
I'm not tempted to drive very fast,
Even when pushed by a jerk.

I can't look at pretty women,
Or even talk to a young child.
Most of us are good people,
But some run totally wild.

People have made bad choices,
Somewhere along the way.
Things we once took for granted,
Are now common, so they say.

Many ignore the taboos of life,
As our morals are in decay.
But is there a better place to be,
Than, in the USA?

A SONGWRITER

Put your words on paper,
You, songwriting man.
Words never sound so good,
When you do the best you can.

We love songs that we can sing along,
Whenever we get the chance.
Some are sung about everyday life,
While others about love and romance.

The best of songs will stay with us,
Down throughout the years.
A few will make us stomp our feet,
With others, we cry some tears.

Songs express the things we feel,
As we work, live, and play.
And songs can put a smile on our face,
As we start a brand new day.

To those who write the magical words,
We'll always love you so.
Were it not for the songs you write,
There would never be a show.

We love to see you up on the stage,
With your band spread side to side.
And to hear you singing your songs,
As the fans show their pride.

TODAY

Today is my day, as the paper read,
And God planned this one for me.
Today, I plan to walk down the aisle,
There for all to see.

Today is the day girls long for.
Today, our lives become one.
Today, you'll take me as your wife,
As we race to the evening sun.

Today, we'll start our lives anew,
And say goodbye to the old.
Today, we'll shake our fists at the devil,
Together, we can be that bold.

Today, we'll be blessed by God,
As our slate will be wiped clean.
Today, we'll show respect for all,
As we face the good times and lean.

Today won't be like all the others,
As some write in their book.
Slowly, we'll turn and walk the aisle,
As family and friends take a look.

Today, I'll promise you all my love,
And today, I'll give you my life.
Today, our future will be before us,
Today I become your wife.

THE LAST GOOD-BYE

We fell in love at a tender age.
Are you sure you want to do this, while turning the page?
We didn't have money for a honeymoon,
But don't you worry - we'll be going real soon.

The military took him one cold day.
He liked it so much, he decided to stay.
We traveled the country for twenty years or so.
Then, one day, he asked me, "Where do you want to go?"

Our last duty station was down on the coast,
We moved once more, where jobs were the most.
The crazy old man tried whatever came along.
And then, one day, he tried writing a song.

I enjoyed all the years that we had together,
Throughout the good times, and bad weather.
As I look back over the many years past,
My only regret is they went so fast.

When's the last time I said good-bye?
As I sit on this bench, I can't remember when.
We've been together for all these years,
And the Lord knows I've shed a million tears.

Well, he's gone now, and I pray to the Father,
That his soul's with Him, and not a place hotter.
He always worried about some things he'd done,
But the Bible assures us; we can leave it to the Son.

DEATH

D eath will come to everyone,
Of that, there's never a doubt.
People have one life to live:
So, cry, laugh, sing, or shout.

Our children have lots of fun
And Lord, we've had our share.
Some know when to draw the line,
Don't you ever take a dare.

The time comes when you become a man,
Tough decisions we make in life.
Think about the choices you'll make,
Including your job and wife.

As adults, we face lots of things
And we deal with them each day.
Only do what you know is right,
And your path will never stray.

Around the age of fifty-plus,
Our bodies begin to change.
Body and mind don't seem to agree,
As they struggle, they set the range.

There comes a time in all of our lives,
To ponder the things we've done.
A few don't worry about life at all.
From death we constantly run.

DO THE RIGHT THING

Have you accomplished your life's plans?
Have you said your last goodbyes?
Not one of us knows one day to the next,
If tomorrow we'll live or die.

Live each day as it might be your last,
Be kind to your wife and friends.
Don't ever leave home or go to bed angry,
Life is short and always ends.

Every soul will be born of woman,
The one chance at life we'll get.
So, don't throw away your precious life,
It's for sure you'll lose that bet.

If you're trying to live a good life,
Keep looking over your shoulder.
Try not to worry when you leave the house,
Each time you'll only get bolder.

It's so much easier to do the right thing,
Than to worry every day and night.
The only gift for a child of Satan,
Is death when he loses the fight.

DRINK SMART

Take a moment and think about life,
Without that beer in your hand.
Wouldn't your life be better off
Without that aluminum can?

When's the last time you can truly say
That you made it without your crutch?
Your mind was clear and you had a thirst,
For some iced tea, coffee, or such.

Do the right thing and limit yourself,
And you'll never drink to excess.
Of the things you can eat, drink, or buy,
You'll always end up with less.

So, drink a beer or a good glass of wine,
Along with your favorite meal.
But don't take a drink one after another,
Children, you could easily kill.

Why would you say, "Let's get drunk,"
When one or two will do?
You should really think long and hard,
As it might just happen to you.

If you take a drink or possibly more,
Give it some thought from the start.
Everybody likes going to a party,
But you should always drink smart.

TIME

There's a time for everything under the sun.
There's a time to walk and a time to run.
Time works against you when you're in a rush,
And time is your friend when the kids hush.

There's time for a run or to walk mountains high.
There's a time to be born and a time yet to die.
Time is a factor when scouts go hiking,
And time is recorded when temps are spiking.

There's a time for birds to spread their wings.
There's a time to play and a time to sing.
Time is extended if a deadline is tight.
Time is held up if the shuttle's not right.

There's a time set aside for things to grow.
There's a time to stop and a time to go.
Time flies quickly when you're on a date,
And mama gets frantic if you come home late.

There's a time for study and a time to learn.
There's a time for working and a time to earn.
There's a time for God, and there's a time to pray,
Spend time on the bible every single day.

Time can ruin lives and control earthly things.
Time adjust music so others can sing.
There's a time set aside for life to end,
When God calls us home; with the angels, He'll send.

LIFE

Life, I think, has been good to you.
You're exactly where you want to be.
If no one can tell you what to do,
Then why are you speaking for me?

It's your life - you dropped your guard,
And a man took advantage of you.
This is my life - you don't have the right.
To do what you're planning to do.

My life began immediately,
I know you remember the night.
My body grows one cell at a time,
To kill me, what gives you the right?

Only a woman can birth a child,
A job no man can do.
Don't play God and do this thing,
As my mother, I'll always love you.

Don't take my life away from me,
I would never do that to you.
Give me a chance to live my life,
As all souls have a right to do.

To take my life because you're afraid,
Is something you'll always regret.
Allow my body to grow each day,
And I promise you'll never forget.

THE HUSH

W e reported to work just like before,
And started a brand-new day.
Before heading out, we got the news,
A friend had passed away.

A hush came over the building,
Then grief filled the room.
The news came without a warning,
The cause we'd learn real soon.

We don't discuss death that often,
It's a subject we don't want to hear.
Most people will choose to ignore it,
If understood, there's nothing to fear.

Our friend's mother came up to us.
To explain the death of her son.
One of twelve that started the business.
We'll miss all his smiles and fun.

Our friend is now with the Father,
His suffering has come to an end.
For those of us who continue to live,
We should strive to live without sin.

Our thoughts are now with his family,
And we're sure they did their best.
But now they can rejoice in knowing,
Their loved one is finally at rest.

OUR VETERANS

We made demands on a KING back then,
It had never been tried before.
All the things we now take for granted,
Were earned from hard-fought wars.

Our veterans have fought in many battles,
In strange and far-off lands.
They went to defend freedom for all,
Many dying by enemy hands.

They fought for us in two great wars,
And others along the way.
Without their selfless sacrifices,
We'd have no freedoms today.

Try and imagine how your life would be,
Had our country lost those wars.
Where do you think you'd be right now,
And would you have far less, or more?

Our veterans are just normal people,
A few accomplished great things.
Many veterans work tirelessly,
Without ever being seen.

Honor our veterans by living your life,
Don't waste it on drugs and the street.
If you're young, old, strong, and free,
There's nothing that you can't beat.

RULES

W hose idea was it, for all these silly rules?
Why should you care if I shoot a deer or two?
Rules have a way of blocking man's progress,
And who likes being told what to do?

Our states have rules about how fast to go,
And cities have rules telling us when to walk.
These crazy rules pop up everywhere we go,
And the rules even tell us when to talk.

There are rules to guide you if you plan to marry.
There are rules to go by if you want to hunt.
Rules even tell us what size fish to catch,
And rules to follow if a cop you confront.

I crossed the road to get a great picture,
But the rules told me I was too close.
I walked to the edge for a better view,
And saw another rule, but that's how it goes.

We have rules telling us when to work,
And rules tell us to sleep at night.
Rules telling us when to go to school,
The rules of war tell us how to fight.

So many rules that control our lives,
But try getting through a day without them.
Jail awaits those who break certain rules.
But do unto others is the one true gem.

RICH OR POOR

All people should have a home,
The good, as well as the bad.
We're not told where to work or live,
For someone to do so would be mad.

Our riches come in many forms,
Get married and base it on love.
What good is money without a friend,
Like God our Father above?

Does it matter if we're rich or poor?
God will accept us, just as we are.
Take your lot and make it yours,
Dig those ditches or become a star.

I'd rather be a simple poor boy,
With people who are true friends.
Than to be a rich boy with money,
Where disappointment never ends.

So, what good is money anyway,
If you can't even have some fun?
If you go somewhere and flaunt it,
You should never walk but run.

Rich or poor, we're all the same,
So why can't we live together?
If one ends up robbing the other
It's assured life won't last forever.

THERE COMES A TIME

There comes a time in every man's life,
When he settles down and takes a wife,
That will love him.

Because only then will he be complete
As a woman is the one thing
That can tame him.

Men act crazy when they're trying to impress,
And get the attention of a woman
That will live with him.

And as strange as it sounds, men become clowns,
And do stupid things
That will attract them.

As soon as they marry and buy a new home,
Weird things happen which comes along,
That can destroy them.

Then your wife says our lives must change
If we're ever going to make it,
To the very end.

So, what do you do when the odds are against you,
And nothing is working
That will help you?

Well, everyone knows women rule the earth,
And if we can change, life will get better
For all of us.

The moral of my story is to listen to your heart,
And do the things that benefit,
the two of us.

PROTECTION

Tasers, batons, and stun guns,
Are the order of the day.
They're used on very bad people,
It looks like they're here to stay.

It's not safe to walk the streets,
Or leave without locking your door.
Thieves can easily rob you blind.
As they would a local store.

People should defend themselves,
From the evils of the land.
Stand up against the wickedness,
Your neighbors won't lend a hand.

Nay-sayers just can't understand,
That a gun can save their lives.
Always have protection around,
People kill with guns and knives.

Protect your family with a weapon,
And keep it hidden away.
Pray to God to protect them daily.
By keeping evil at bay.

To keep your family safe at night
You should always have a gun.
The one thing you can count on
Is that evil will always have one.

A TIME LONG AGO

My favorite songs take me back,
to a time long ago.
Just young kids with energy to burn,
When they played, "Go cat go."

I thought the slow dance would never die.
But it had slowly reached its prime.
Rock & Roll music was now the rage,
And was played time after time.

Many singers had songs to sing,
And we loved them, everyone.
So, why'd they allow booze and drugs,
Take them before they were done?

When called, there was no answer,
As their lives were taken away.
Jimmy, Janis, Elvis, and others
Had performed their very last day.

Their music would last forever,
Good songs will always survive.
Without knowledge of their passing,
You'd think they were still alive.

No, there's not a Rock & Roll heaven,
As people have sung about.
But maybe one day, far, far away,
We'll hear them as they sing and shout.

A LIFE TO REMEMBER

I'm writing this letter to you, my love,
On the eve of our sixty-eighth year.
When I consider the things we've done
And the memories, I hold so dear.

I think of the way we got our start,
Made our plans, and ran away.
What a chance we took back then,
But it lasted these many days.

I remember our two little children,
The tears, the laughter, and the pain.
All the trials they put us through,
I'd still do it over again.

I also remember the exciting places,
My job required us to go.
And all the thrilling things we did,
The less fortunate will never know.

Time has erased so many names,
Of friends we met along the way.
Much richer for having met them,
And new ones we see each day.

Just goes to show what love can do,
When it's exercised now and then.
I've loved you all these many years,
And I'll love you to the very end.

THE YELLOW JACKETS

There was a team called the Dolphins,
A team that plays football.
Their best year was the '72 season,
The year they took it all.

That's very rare for a football team,
To win every game of the year.
When the Dolphins won the Super Bowl,
You could hear the deafening cheer.

Now, go back one decade more.
To the year of '62.
When a North Carolina high school team
Did what the Dolphins couldn't do.

The team was known as the Yellow Jackets,
From a place called Elizabethtown.
When the lights came on the playing field,
No opponent could take them down.

One team after another stepped up,
Yet, all would fail their test.
Four straight years as state champions
With a perfect season, their best.

A perfect season is very rare,
Still harder to go undefeated.
Large crowds came to see them play,
And the coach was never unseated.

AN ANGRY YOUNG MAN

There was something in the air,
The morning she was running late.
When the drunk ran them in the river,
They were victims of fate.

Everyone knew the story,
Of his wife and little girl.
When the jury gave its decision
He gave up on the world.

Down at the bend of the river,
There's an angry young man.
Headed down the road to nowhere,
Fast as he can.

He lost all respect for the people,
If you spoke, he just put you down.
They crossed the street to avoid him,
And kept praying that he'd leave town.

Feared all over the county,
Never looked a soul in the eye.
If he ever got word, you crossed him.
You were put on a list to die.

Headed down in the river,
There's an angry young man.
Headed down the road to nowhere,
Fast as he can.

Finally, one day it happened,
The fears were coming true.
There were people dying,
And nothing the sheriff could do.

You could hear the eerie silence.
As he drove toward the town.
He was forced off the bridge,
And his bones never found.

Down on the bottom of the river
Lay the bones of an angry young man.
Headed down the road to nowhere,
Never to be seen again.

Ooau, down on the bottom of the river,
Lay the bones of an angry young man.
Headed down the road to nowhere,
Never to be found again.

Yea, Yea, never to be found again.
Angry young man.

CAROLINA BEACH

I was sitting on the sand at Carolina Beach
Wishing I was back home.
Sitting on the beach till the sun comes up,
I never liked being alone.

I'm going to Carolina for a summer break,
Gonna leave my job today.
I never expected the message I got,
How could anyone treat me that way?

We've been together for six long years,
We were always on the go.
So, what'da you do when they act this way?
You try not to put on a show.

Sittin' on the sand at Carolina Beach
Wishin' I was back home.
Sittin' on the beach till the sun comes up
I never liked being alone.

I saw a man jogging down the beach,
And he was staring at me.
I wiped a tear away from my eyes,
As he walked on over to see.

His words were kind as he talked to me,
He was a breath of fresh air.
He seemed to care about the things I said,
And I loved his curly blonde hair.

We sat on the beach till the sun came up,
Still having lots to say.
We both agreed that we should meet again,
As he stood up and jogged away.

I'm sittin' on the sand at Carolina Beach
Wishing I was back home.
My boyfriend said he was leaving me,
Never thought about being alone.

We've been together for six long years,
We were always on the go.
So, what'da you do when they act this way?
You try not to put on a show.

We sat on the beach till the sun came up,
Still having lots to say.
We both agreed we should meet again,
As he stood up and jogged away.

I was sitting on the sand at Carolina Beach
Wishing I was back home.
Sitting on the beach till the sun comes up,
I never liked being alone.

We sat on the beach till the sun came up,
Still having lots to say.
We both agreed we should meet again,
As he stood up and jogged away.

So, we both agreed we should meet again,
As he stood up and jogged away.

PLEASE DON'T CRY

Your heart was broken today.
He's taken your plans away.
He let you down again,
With time your heart will mend.

So, please don't cry anymore.
Please don't cry anymore.
There'll come a day when your tears will fade.
You'll see the choices you made weren't the best for you.

I think girl you'd do it different today,
By never letting anyone take yours dreams away.
Please don't cry anymore.
He's not the man you thought you knew

And everything he did hurt you.
When his cheating went too far,
He began to see who you really are.
So, please don't cry anymore.

Please don't cry anymore.

There'll come a day when your tears will fade.
You'll see the choices you made weren't the best for you.
I think girl you'd do it different today,
By never letting anyone take yours dreams away.

So, please don't cry anymore.

How you struggled to get past him,
And you could have your choice of men.
You can face life with with your pride,
And I'll be there when you're ready to decide.

So, please don't cry anymore.
Please don't cry anymore.

The day has come for your tears to fade.
This time the choice you made was the best for you.
Together we'll do things different today,
By never letting anyone take yours dreams away.

So, please don cry anymore.
No! Please don't cry anymore.

A MAN CALLED JESUS

I know a man called Jesus,
He loves us one and all.
He came to Earth to save our souls,
And people now stand tall.

I love a man called Jesus,
He walked on earth one day.
He lived and died for all mankind,
And now we proudly say.

I love a man called Jesus,
He healed the sick and lame.
They left their homes and walked the miles,
From everywhere, they came.

I know a man called Jesus,
He preached the word to men.
And one by one, they came to him,
With hope and outreached hands.

I love a man called Jesus,
They tested Him one day.
He came to Earth to save mankind.
But this time He wouldn't stay.

His earthly father was Joseph,
The heavenly was God,
Each man would teach Him many things.
The devil He would trod.

I know a man called Jesus,
He came to change the world.
His plan would take so many years
Before it would unfurl.

I know a man called Jesus,
He died on Calvary.
But one day soon He'll reappear,
For all the world to see.
I know a man called Jesus.

MY PRECIOUS ANGEL

Close your eyes, my little darlin'.
And your fears will slip away.
Go to sleep, my precious angel,
'Cause your mama's here to stay.

Lay your head on my shoulders,
Close your eyes to morning, then.
You look so sweet and lovely,
Come and join your furry friend.

Close your eyes, my little darlin'.
And your fears will slip away.
Go to sleep, my precious angel,
'Cause your mama's here to stay.

As you sleep, my sweet angel,
I'll sing a song just for you.
As you lay in restful slumber
Don't you worry, I'm here for you.

Close your eyes, my little darlin'
And your fears will slip away.
Go to sleep, my precious angel,
'Cause your mama's here to stay.

So go to sleep, my little darlin'.
You can dream, a dream or two.
And when you wake up tomorrow,
I'll be waiting here for you.

Close your eyes, my little darlin'.
And your fears will slip away.
Go to sleep, my precious angel,
'Cause your mama's here to stay,

Yea, your mama's here to stay.

MY ONE TRUE LOVE

A friend of ours once knew told me a story,
Of a time you were thinking of me.
That you were crying at a party where
You and I happened to be.

I failed to control my body's desires,
Made love to your very best friend.
One day she threatened to tell you a story,
An affair I put to an end.

How many times have I dreamed of you
Or thought about calling by phone?
I'm so, so tired of living this lie,
We need to have time alone.

I'd love to tell you the number of times,
That you have crossed my mind.
And if we could sit and talk it over,
I'm sure things will be just fine.

I'd tell you that I think of you always,
And I cherish the times we had.
I hate the day I forced you to leave,
And the mistake that was oh-so-bad.

She forced me to leave my one true love,
Who I think about every day.
She had to destroy the love we shared.
Won't you come back to me, I pray?

So yes, you're still my one true love,
I can't change the mistake I made.
What's done is done but I promise you this,
That our love will never fade.

CALL ON ME

I heard about you from a friend of mine,
Who told me of the life you live,
And about the man that married you,
And now he takes but never gives.

Your friends knew he wasn't right for you,
And they told you from the very start.
That He was no good a running around,
And he left you with a broken heart.

If you call on me, I'm gonna come to you,
I'm gonna hold you tight and take away your blues.
If you call on me, I'll help you out of the rut
That he's been putting you through, I know it's rough.

When times are tough and the nights are lonely,
I'll put you at ease if you call on me.
But when he's drunk and takes it out on you
I can turn it around.

Call on me, I'll be there for you
When you make that call, you're gonna see
What it feels like to be loved by a man,
Who will gladly give you all the love he can.

If you call on me, I'm gonna come to you.
I'm gonna hold you tight and take away your blues.
If you call on me, I'll help you out of the rut
That he's been putting you through, I know it's rough.

The man you married keeps pulling you down,
But you can stop him cold if you call on me.
When you call on me I'm gonna take him down
Down to the point that he'll beg to leave town.

Music Break

If you take control of your life again,
You can rise above it if you call on me.
If you call on me, I'm gonna come to you.
I'm gonna hold you tight and take away your blues.

If you call on me, I'll help you out of the rut
That he's been putting you through, I know it's rough.
Tell me true he's not the man of your dreams;
You deserve much better or so it seems.

And at that point you have to tell me true,
If there's ever going to be a me and you -
If there's ever going to be a me and you -
If there's ever going to be a me and you -

Oh, oh, ummm.

MAMA TOLD ME

As I left for work like I'd always done before
I ran in to him as I stepped out the door.
I knocked him to the ground, we were both on the phone,
Tried picking him up because he was alone.

Mama told me there'd be some days like this.
It started with hello and would end with a kiss.
My mind started racing, would he ask me for a date?
And I had to work fast or to work I'd be late.

Good God Almighty what a good-looking lad!
But I should keep on walking
Or I'll do something bad.
So, keep your pants on, Dolly
Like your mama said to do.
Keep your pants on, Dolly
Or he'll end up hurting you.

He stopped me for a minute as I opened the door,
So, I gave him my number, now I'll see what's in store.
I'll be listening to the phone as I wait for his call,
He was oh, so dreamy, and for me, not that tall.

It's been a week or so, not a word from him,
It's a cool Saturday morning, and I'm walking to the gym.
When I leave for home, I see him crossing the street.
And my stomach is turning, as we're destined to meet.

Good God Almighty what a good-looking lad!
But I should keep on walking
Or I'll do something bad.
So, keep your pants on, Dolly
Like your mama said to do.
Keep your pants on, Dolly
Or he'll end up hurting you.

Why he never called, he said my number he lost.
So, I let him walk me home as I thought about the cost.
Now we've dated each other for a year and more.
And we're doing alright, 'cause it's him I adore.

After working up the courage, he finally gave me a ring.
And when I took a good look, I just had to dance and sing.
Now, what should I say as he gets on his knee?
It was, "Yes! Yes! Yes!" Now you can come home with me.

Good God Almighty what a good-looking lad!
But I should keep on walking
Or I'll do something bad.
So, keep your pants on, Dolly
Like your mama said to do.
Keep your pants on, Dolly
Or he'll end up hurting you.

THE DAYS OF LONG AGO

In the days of long ago
I'm reminded of a time.
When we would go sit by a stream
As we listened to the church bells chime.

Holding hands was just the start.
We knew our lives were so.
Kissing, hugging, and making plans
In the days of long ago.

Young, I know we were young back then,
Convinced we could make the world grow.
Naive? Maybe, but so much in love,
In the days of long ago.

In the days of long ago,
Life was good and oh-so-sweet.
There was nothing we couldn't do
With the world at our feet.

We thought we knew it all back then,
What a difference we could make,
In a world such as the one we had.
We just couldn't make a mistake.

We were so ready to take on the world,
And we had our dreams back then.
We thought we could do anything then,
In the days of long ago.

Life was so much easier then,
And love was in the air back then.
As each of us made our plans, then,
To leave our homes, family, and friends.

In those days of long ago.
Da, da, da, da, da
De, de, de, de, de,
Da, da, da, da, da
Da, da, da, da, da,
De, de, de, de, de
In those days of long ago.

GOING FISHING

As I walked to the front door, she turned around to see
My hand touch the doorknob that's it for you and me.
I'm so tired of you flirting with the men here in town.
And I'm tired of the hurting - from you dragging me down.

So tell me, how - and when - did our love go so wrong?
Boy, were we wild back then.
And what we had together was as rare as it could be.
Will I ever find true love again?

I want - to have - some fun of my own
Going fishing and hang with the guys.
Cause I'm free to go and do as I please
I want to reach up and touch the sky.

Instrumental break.

Nevermore will I argue - or fight.
If I go down that road - again.
And I'm going to make sure to do things right.
I'll be a husband - as well as a friend.

So tell me, how - and when - did our love go so wrong?
Boy, were we wild back then.
And what we had together was as rare as it could be
Will I ever find true love again?

Yes, I want - to have - some fun of my own
Going fishing and hang with the guys.
Cause I'm free to go and do as I please
I want to reach up and touch the sky.

Yes, I'm free to go - and do as I please.
I want to reach up and touch the sky.
I want to reach up and touch the sky.
I'm going to reach up - and touch the sky.

ABOUT THE AUTHOR

JERRY D. JACKSON was brought into this world in the small country town of Elizabethtown, NC, on 16 August 1946. He graduated from high school in June of 1965, got married, fathered a child, went on active military duty, completed two specialized schools, and served a year in Vietnam, all before his twenty-first birthday. Later, he completed a two-year class through George Washington University, finishing second in his class, and in 1976, he graduated from the Coast Guard Officer Candidate School located in historic Yorktown, Virginia, and went on to complete over twenty-three years of service defending his country with pride. Jerry and his late wife started a furniture business in Mt. Juliet, TN., in 1986. This decorated veteran of the United States Coast Guard retired from active military service with the rank of Lieutenant (03), and retired in September of 1986.

All of his childhood experiences, growing up in the country, and his many experiences during and after his military service contributed greatly to the poems found in this book. Mr. Jackson continues to write and is a Deacon at a church he attends every Sunday.